BRIGHTON'S TRAMWAYS

Robert J Harley

MP Middleton Press

Cover picture: This photograph was taken on the occasion of an enthusiasts tour of Brighton on 1st September 1938, exactly one year before the system closed. The tram containing all the Light Railway Transport League devotees is positioned at the end of the Queen's Road track. The colours used on the covers are similar to those employed by the Corporation on its tramcars. (D.W.K.Jones)

First published October 1992

ISBN 1 873793 02 2

© Middleton Press 1992

Design - Deborah Goodridge

Published by Middleton Press
        Easebourne Lane
        Midhurst
        West Sussex
        GU29 9AZ
        Tel: (0730) 813169

Printed & bound by Biddles Ltd,
        Guildford and Kings Lynn

CONTENTS

GEOGRAPHICAL SETTING

Brighton and the neighbouring towns of Hove and Shoreham lie on the South Coast of England in the county of Sussex. London is situated to the north about 50 miles or 80 kms. distant. Along the Channel sea shore the beach is mostly pebbles kept in check by numerous groynes and breakwaters against the force of winter storms which can be severe. Away from the seashore, the land rises steeply to the north and east in a series of ridges which form part of the South Downs. Thus in a very short distance a height of almost 650 feet/200 metres above sea level is reached. This high ground forms the coast to the east of Brighton in a line of chalk cliffs broken by river valleys and inlets.

INTRODUCTION AND ACKNOWLEDGEMENTS

This book is the first in a series entitled "Tramway Classics". I have tried to portray in pictures and in text the fascinating story of the horse, steam, cable and electric tramways in the area. Fortunately all is not lost today, and the Volk's Electric Railway is still with us after more than a century of operation.

Unless otherwise stated, all the maps used in this book are 25ins to 1 mile (1:2500. scale), published in 1898. Readers will also note that I have included metric equivalent measurements where possible, this will help model makers and fellow tramway enthusiasts in other countries. Of course, during the tram era in Brighton imperial weights and measures were used exclusively.

The research for this work on Brighton Tramways has been greatly assisted by a number of individuals who have collected the photographs and postcards used in this book. I wish to record my thanks to Nick Kelly, an acknowledged expert on the Brighton and Shoreham line, also to Ray Tabraham and Alan Watkins who have allowed me to dip into their extensive collections. Much help has been given by G.Baddeley, J.Baker, J.Blackwell, B.Boddy, P.Booth, C.Carter, S.Cole, J.C.Gillham, P.Hay, W.J.Haynes, D.W.K.Jones, M.A.Kelly, E.R.Oakley, and my fellow members of the Tramway and Light Railway Society, Sussex Area. A special vote of gratitude goes to Bob Elliston of Eastbourne and Don Thompson of Whetstone, both of whom received me so cordially into their homes. I must pay tribute to the drawing skills of Father John Bolton of Worth Abbey, whose expertise has enriched this work. Thanks are also due to Vic Mitchell and the Middleton Press for their encouragement in the preparation of this series. Finally, to my long suffering wife Janet, a big thank you for all the support during this project.

HISTORICAL BACKGROUND

The first street tramway to open in the Brighton area was the line from Southdown Road, Shoreham to the Hove boundary at Westbourne Villas, serving Shoreham Station, Southwick, Portslade and New Church Road. Construction started in 1883 and the line was opened with steam traction on 3rd July 1884. Passenger traffic did not live up to expectations, the section west of Shoreham Station operated by a single tram closed in 1887. Experiments were conducted with other forms of mechanical traction. An Elieson battery electric locomotive was tested and found wanting, indeed, horse power took over the whole service and the remaining steam trams were sold to Wigan in 1893. Control of the company passed to the BET.- the British Electric Traction Co.- in 1898, but all the subsequent schemes for electrification and through services from Worthing to Brighton came to nothing. This was mainly due to the intransigence of the local authorities particularly Hove where the idea of rails in the streets met with a hostile reaction. The Brighton and Shoreham horse tramway was thus easy prey to the motor bus and operations ceased on 6th June 1913.

Magnus Volk was born in Brighton in 1851. He was one of the most talented inventors of the late Victorian age and his legacy to posterity is the Volk's Electric Railway which was opened in 1883 and is still running today. The line originally extended from the Swimming Arch (near the Aquarium) to the Old Chain Pier; the motive power was a two axle car built to a track gauge of 2ft/610mm and capable of holding ten passengers. The line was extended in 1884 and the gauge converted to 2ft 9ins/838mm, although subsequently this was reduced by half an inch. Athough not strictly a street tramway, the technology of the VER was to prove an inspiration for the succeeding generation of electric vehicles. The idea of extending along the coast to Rottingdean proved irresistible to Magnus Volk, however a conventional line would have entailed large and expensive engineering works through the chalk cliffs. He got to work devising a unique marine tramway where the

rails would actually be laid on the sea bed. The Brighton and Rottingdean Seashore Electric Tramroad opened in November 1896, its Brighton terminus being the Banjo Groyne. The service lasted a few days before disaster struck in early December when severe storms wrecked the whole outfit. Undaunted, Volk set about reconstruction for a re-opening date of July 1897 and the one tramcar named "Pioneer" was launched again to continue a career which lasted until the turn of the century. The operation was never profitable and a decision by Brighton Corporation to build a number of coastal defence breakwaters across its path was the final straw. The line was finally dismantled around 1910, leaving the concrete sleeper blocks as mute witness during low tide to an ingenious, if rather impractical form of transport.

Brighton Corporation Tramways opened on 25th November 1901, with a fleet of traditional four-wheel open top double deck trams to a gauge of 3ft 6ins/1067mm. At its fullest extent in 1904 routes were operated to Lewes Road, Seven Dials and Dyke Road, Preston Drove via Ditchling Road and Beaconsfield Villas, Central Station, Race Hill, and Queen's Park. The Aquarium terminus was the hub of the system with frequent departures to other parts of town. Throughout its existence the Tramways Department was famed for the car rebuilding programme, so that in 1927 the manager could claim that "all cars now running have been built on these premises." However, the two axle, open top design was retained and this became increasingly anachronistic during the late thirties when advances in motor bus and trolleybus technology made for a more attractive mode of town transport. The bulk of the Brighton system was replaced by trolleybuses in 1939, the last car entering the depot in Lewes Road in the early hours of 1st September 1939, two days before a much greater event overtook the Nation. The rails were speedily removed for wartime scrap and the most obvious relics of the tramway era are several passenger shelters which still serve the needs of the travelling public.

● BRIGHTON AND SHOREHAM TRAMWAY ●

1. Our journey along the Brighton and Shoreham Tramway starts appropriately at the western terminus outside the Burrell Arms, Shoreham. In 1897 a double deck, two horse tram is about to leave for Portslade. Some of the passengers may have arrived by train at Shoreham Station which lies behind the inn. Obviously a bracing ride on the top deck along the front was a pleasure which the main line LBSCR could not match. (N.Kelly Coll.)

BRIGHTON & SHOREHAM TRAMWAY - 1884-1913

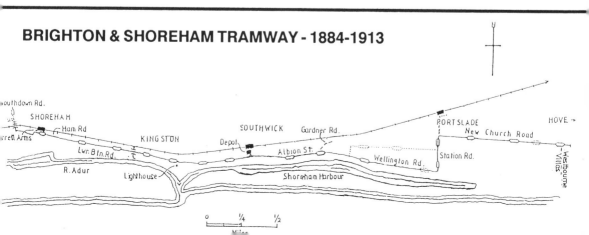

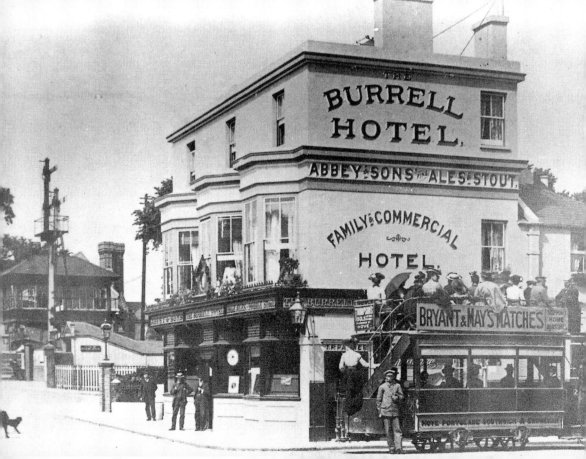

2. A fine Summer's day in 1905. Some ladies have chosen to protect themselves from the noonday sun under the shelter of a parasol. A little boy stands and watches as the conductor comes round the rear of the car ready to give the starting signal to the driver. Then with a gentle pull of the reins and a brisk call of "walk on", the tram will sway forward over the points of the passing loop to amble peacefully along Ham Road towards open country and the River Adur estuary. (N.Kelly Coll.)

3. At the Burrell Hotel again, this is a fine study of car 12 caught by the camera in the Summer of 1905. Both driver and conductor are featured together with almost a full load of passengers decked out in their Edwardian finery. Notice the marvellous array of hats which were "de rigueur" for a day out by the seaside. (N.Kelly Coll.)

4. A close up of the previous picture; the tram is now lettered Hove, Portslade, Southwick and Shoreham. The prospect of successfully gaining access to Brighton was now a very remote one due to the intransigence of Hove Council. (N.Kelly Coll.)

5. Car 11 at the Shoreham terminus. This view
and the one following were surely a set for the
album of the gentlemen standing by the tram.
The reader may be able to guess who took each
shot! Notice the garden or transverse seats on
the top deck and the ladies in the lower saloon
occupying the longitudinal benches next to the
windows. (N.Kelly Coll.)

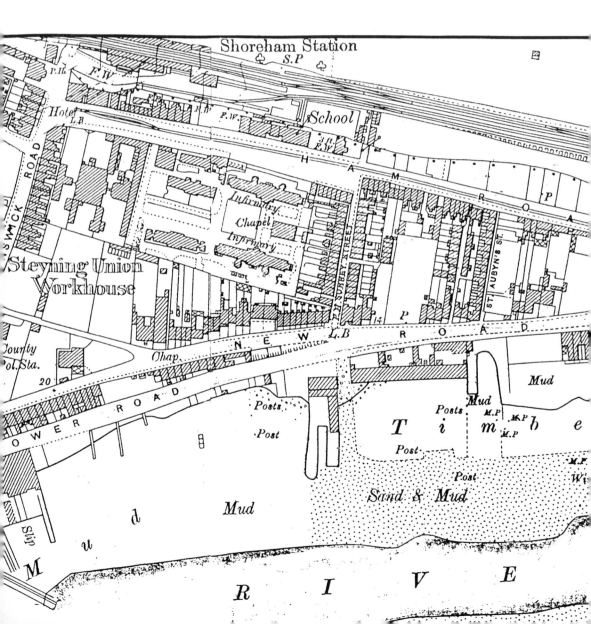

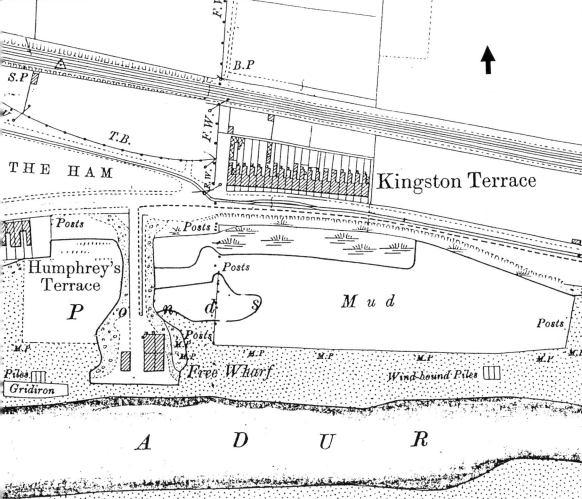

6. A few minutes later. By this time the horses must have become a little restless, so the conductor has positioned himself to prevent any undignified departure. (N.Kelly Coll.)

7. A wreath is hanging on car 10 as a valedictory gesture. The occasion is the last tram from Shoreham on 6th June 1913. On the side is the "wheel and magnet" emblem of the British Electric Traction Co., which had decided to cut its losses and abandon the line. The youthful conductor is Albert James who had left school the previous Christmas at the age of 14 to work alongside Ben Fears, the driver, pictured next to him. Unfortunately after this 6.45 p.m. departure, both would be out of a job, as would Mr.Newcombe the Tramway Manager, standing on the far right of the picture. The short canopies of the car roof are explained by the fact that this tram had been cut down to a single decker in 1910; large vehicles were no longer needed as the competing motor buses swallowed up all the traffic. (N.Kelly Coll.)

8. Ham Road School, Shoreham is passed by car 7 built by Oldbury in 1886. Before the turn of the century (this photo dates from about 1898) the tramway was very much the "king of the road" with few other vehicles to challenge its position. (N.Kelly Coll.)

9. We continue our journey towards Hove by pausing with car 12 at the passing loop opposite Kingston Terrace. The driver and conductor had plenty of time in 1907 to stop in the middle of the highway for the photographer to record them. The gentleman on the top deck with the pipe reminds us that smoking was only permitted on the outside of the trams. (N.Kelly Coll.)

10. Further eastwards we travel, past the harbour wharves and a malthouse, till we reach the Pier Terrace, Custom House passing loop pictured here. Just to the right of this 1910 view is the famous High Lighthouse, which was the model for the design on the old penny coin next to the seated Britannia. (N.Kelly Coll.)

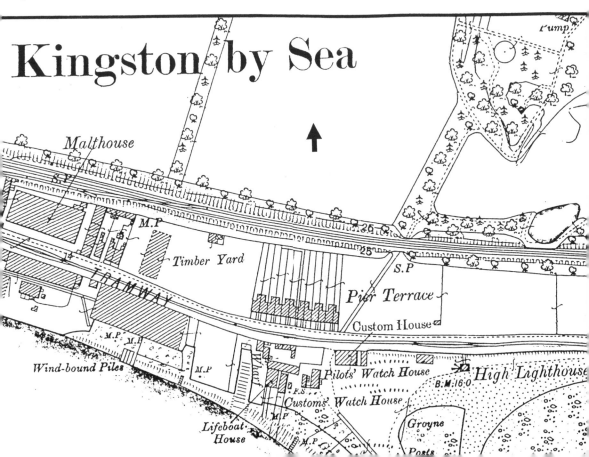

Kingston by Sea

Malthouse

Timber Yard

TRAMWAY

M.P

S.P

Pier Terrace

Custom House

Pump

Wind-bound Piles

Pilots' Watch House

Customs' Watch House

High Lighthouse

B.M:16.0

Groyne

Lifeboat House

Posts

11. Albion Street, Southwick, "en fete" for the Diamond Jubilee of Queen Victoria in 1897. In the centre of this animated scene is car 4 built in 1891, pursued by a father guiding his son on a pony, whilst the flags of the Union and the Empire flutter overhead. Outside Southwick Post Office, postmen have gathered in the sunshine to watch the photographer. In front of the tram a horse and cart are passing the entrance to the depot just by the Methodist Chapel. The whole event would have offered a welcome relief to many from the poverty which they experienced in their daily lives.
(N.Kelly Coll)

12. On the other side of Albion Street, this time in 1913, car 10 stops outside Courtney and Birkett, the shipwrights. Aside from nautical activities, the firm had also constructed the Devil's Dyke Funicular Railway in 1897. However, by the time of this view, when the gentleman with the spaniel had come across from the depot to pose in front of the tram, the steep grade railway had already failed.
(N.Kelly Coll)

13. Outside the depot in Albion Street the very last tram halts before disappearing from the Sussex roads for ever. In the background is the Seahouse Shades pub which had a reputation for bar room brawls rivalling that of the Wild West. (N.Kelly Coll.)

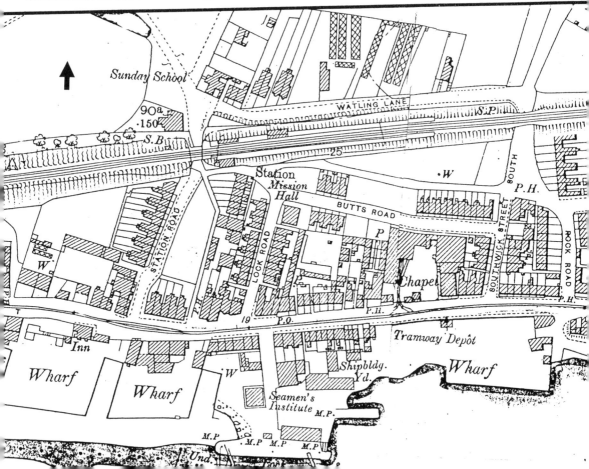

14. The last car in the depot. The tram was painted in the BET standard livery of dark lake and cream. (N.Kelly Coll.)

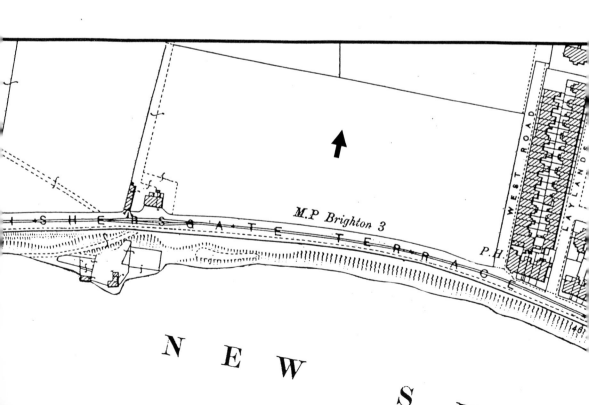

M.P Brighton 3

SHEEPSGATE TERRACE

WEST ROAD

LAYLANDS

P.H

N E W S

15. The route from Southwick to Fishersgate crossed open country. Here we see car 5 trundling sedately along the road in 1897. (N.Kelly Coll.)

16. The last tram pauses on the loop in Fishersgate Terrace. On the dash of the car near the horse's hind legs is the ratchet and pawl handbrake, with the chain wound round the bottom of the vertical brass rod. (N.Kelly Coll.)

17. A smiling Ben Fears urges the team onwards, climbing Wellington Road, Portslade, opposite Middle Street. In the background is the steam driven Britannia Flour Mills. (N.Kelly Coll.)

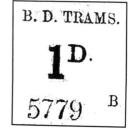

B. D. TRAMS.

1D.

5779 B

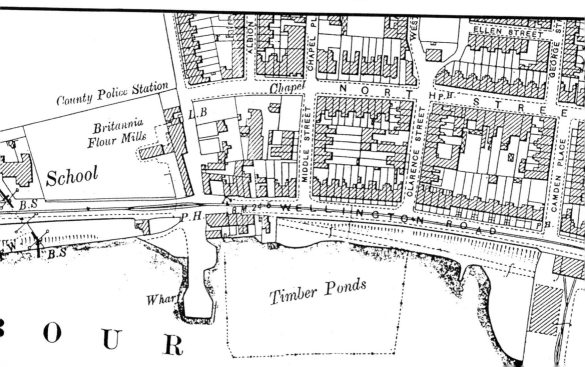

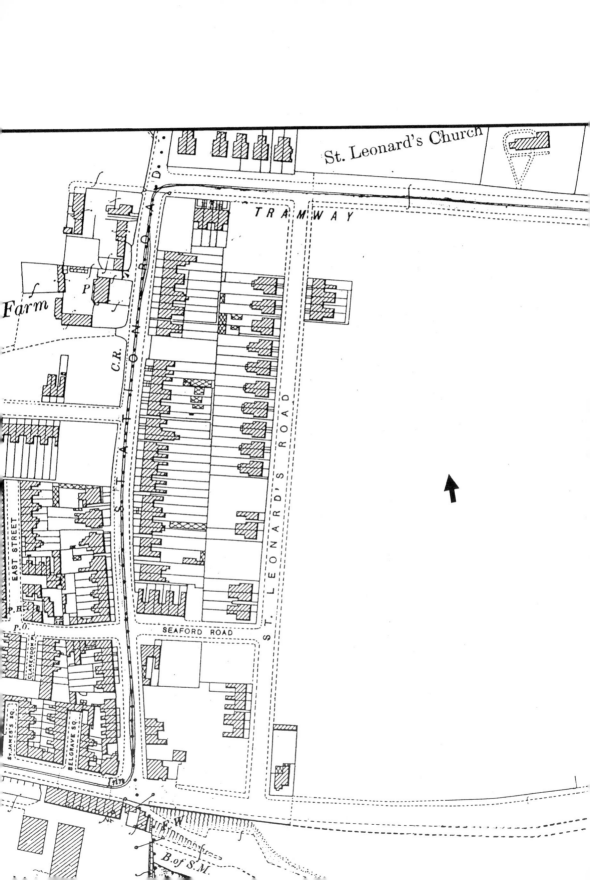

St. Leonard's Church

Farm

TRAMWAY

ST. LEONARD'S ROAD

EAST STREET

SEAFORD ROAD

ST. JAMES'S SQ.

BELGRAVE SQ.

CLARENDON P.

P.H.

P.O.

Inn

18. After passing through the village of Portslade-by-Sea the tramway continued along New Church Road which at the time was very little developed, to terminate at the Hove boundary opposite Westbourne Villas. In this 1897 view, car 4 is travelling in a westerly direction towards Portslade. (N.Kelly Coll.)

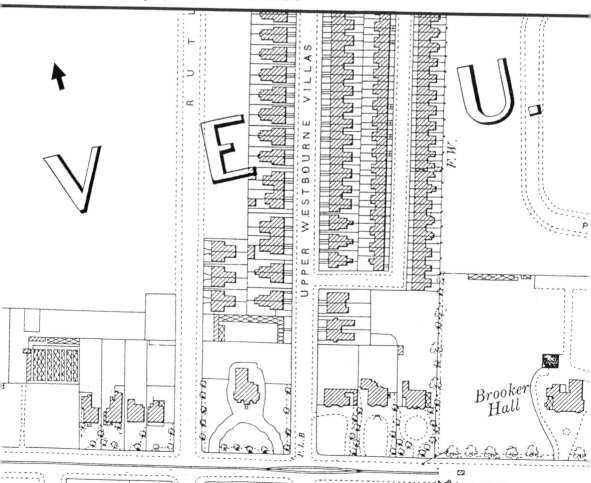

19. Finally we reach the end of the line, quite literally in this case, since the date is 23rd October 1912, the last day of the New Church Road service to Portslade. Car 10, pictured here, will also perform the final rites on the rest of the line the following Summer. With an almost indecent haste minutes after the last car left, Hove Council workmen descended on the road to rip up the hated tramtrack, unfortunately they then made such a mess of reconstructing the highway that this was the subject of local complaint for many months to come. (N.Kelly Coll.)

20. Whereas the previous picture had caused sadness for some, this fine scene of Wilkinson locomotive 2 and Falcon passenger car is witness to the opposite emotion. This is 1884 and the world for the Brighton and Shoreham promoters must have seemed rich with possibilities. Little did they think, when this photo was posed at Westbourne Villas, that this point would remain the terminus until the end of operations. (N.Kelly Coll.)

21. Car 2 worked between Hove and Portslade and is pictured in New Church Road around 1897. Unusually for the time, this car has a vestibule windscreen protection at either end of the car. Some London electric trams were still running with open platforms as late as 1940! (N.Kelly Coll.)

22. The tramway never did cross Hove to reach Brighton, passengers had to change at the boundary to this connecting horse bus 112 of the Brighton and Preston United Omnibus Company. Soon motor buses would cover the whole route to Shoreham and the tramway would be doomed. (N.Kelly Coll.)

ROLLING STOCK

23. The two Brighton and Shoreham vertical boiler steam locos, which were built by William Wilkinson of Wigan, worked on the south coast from 1884 to 1893, when they were sold to Wigan District Tramways in Lancashire. One is pictured here in its second home. At Brighton the locos were painted dark brown and cream. (N.Kelly Coll.)

24. This Aveling and Porter steam tram loco worked on the line from 1887 to 1889. The engine was constructed at the Invicta Works, Rochester, Kent and bears the county crest in this contemporary engraving. For those of a more technical disposition, the sectional elevations show the fascinating arrangement of boiler, pistons, cylinders and connecting rods necessary for generating the power to pull a loaded tramway car along the highway.

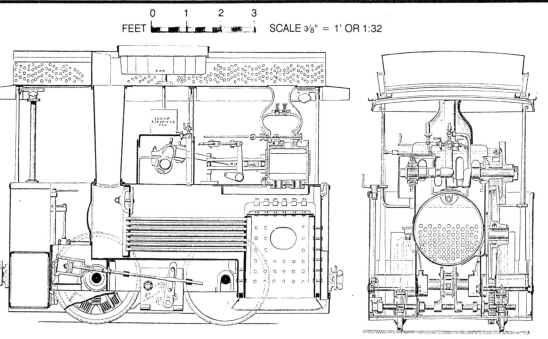

```
        0    1    2    3
FEET ┣━━┿━━┿━━┥         SCALE ⅜" = 1' OR 1:32
```

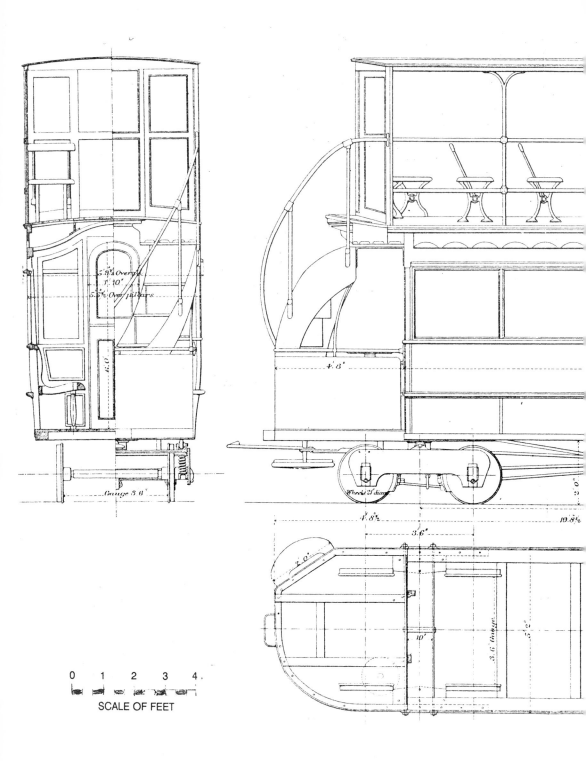

5.9½ Overall
1′ 10″
5.6½ Over pillars

6.0″

Gauge 3.6″

4.6″

Wheels 2′ diam.

2.0″

4.8½   19.8½

3.6

2.0″

10′   3.6 Gauge   5.2″

0 1 2 3 4
SCALE OF FEET

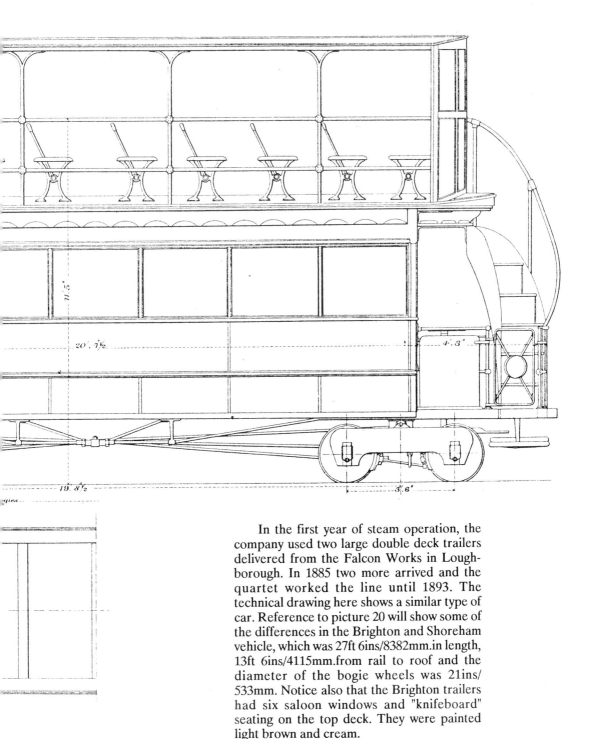

In the first year of steam operation, the company used two large double deck trailers delivered from the Falcon Works in Loughborough. In 1885 two more arrived and the quartet worked the line until 1893. The technical drawing here shows a similar type of car. Reference to picture 20 will show some of the differences in the Brighton and Shoreham vehicle, which was 27ft 6ins/8382mm.in length, 13ft 6ins/4115mm.from rail to roof and the diameter of the bogie wheels was 21ins/533mm. Notice also that the Brighton trailers had six saloon windows and "knifeboard" seating on the top deck. They were painted light brown and cream.
(R.J.Harley Coll., from D.K.Clark, "Tramways, Their Construction and Working.")

This detailed drawing appeared in "Engineering." The railway was built by Courtney and Birkett of Southwick, who also had a maintenance contract with the Brighton and Shoreham Tramway.

Elevation of Car

Elevation for Cutting

6'6" Pile

1/4 Plates

Channel Steel C's 2¼ x ¼

2' 9"

Section at Rail Joint

2' 4"

Section of Rail

Two Spikes thus Every 3 ft

2 Fang Bolts thus every 10 ft

Tie Rod ¾ Dia 4' 0 Long

Cast Iron Pipe ¾ Int'l Diar ¼ Thick 2' 6" Wide

Elevation of Roller

Side Elevation

Elevation

Rail Joint

Longitudinal Sleepers

Rails 30 feet Long

6'6" Piles

Cutting

Section

2' 4"

Plan of Surface

6'6" Piles

THE DEVIL'S DYKE RAILWAY, BRIGHTON

MR. CHARLES O. BLABER, ASSOC. M.I.C.E., ENGINEER

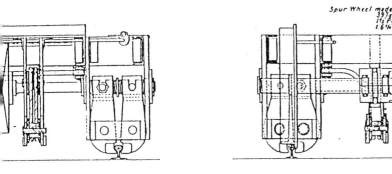

Spur Wheel made in Halves with Male Clutch & Bolted Together.
39 Teeth
1½ Pitch
1.6¼ Pitch Dia.

Section B.A.

Section A.D.

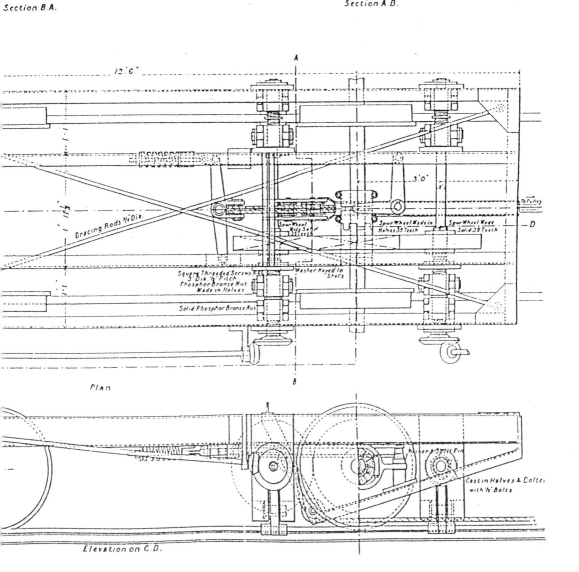

12'6"

A

3'0"

To Pulley

— D

Bracing Rods ¾ Dia.

Spur Wheel Made in Halves 39 Teeth

Spur Wheel Made Solid 39 Teeth

Spur Wheel Keyed Solid

Square Threaded Screws 3 Dia. ½ Pitch
Phosphor Bronze Nut Made in Halves

Washer Keyed to Shaft

Solid Phosphor Bronze Nut

Plan

B

Cast in Halves & Bolted with ⅞ Bolts

Elevation on C.D.

25. The Brighton and Shoreham may have ended its days as a relic, but it should be remembered that it served a useful purpose as a test bed for new forms of mechanical traction. In July and August of 1887 C.P.Elieson ran his pioneer battery electric locomotive , a prototype of which is pictured here on the North Metropolitan Tramways in London the previous year. (N.Kelly Coll.)

26. The Devil's Dyke line opened on 24th July 1897; it was built to save visitors the steep walk up the Downs. Unfortunately, traffic did not live up to expectations. The writer on the back of this postcard view, which was sent in September 1909, records that the line had already closed as it was too dangerous. Cable traction was also used on a short lived line built by Magnus Volk in early 1884. The railway was constructed down the west stairway leading to Paston Place. It was a water balance funicular, and there is some doubt whether it opened for public use; it only worked during March, April and May of 1884. (R.J.Harley Coll.)

• BRIGHTON CORPORATION TRAMWAYS •

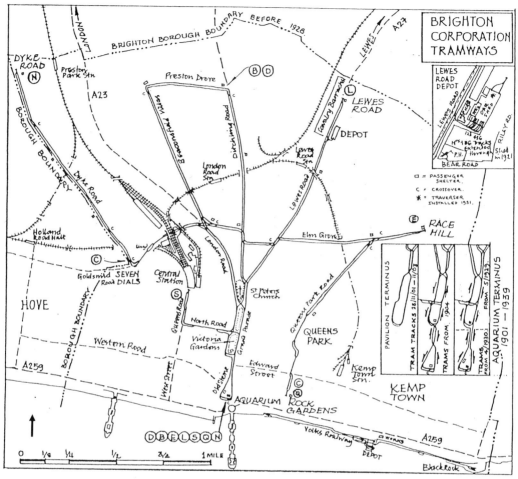

Final track layout of Brighton Corporation Tramways at its fullest extent in 1938. Drawn by Fr. John Bolton based on information from Ray Tabraham and J.C. Gillham.

1935-36.

BRIGHTON CORPORATION TRAMWAYS

ROUTE	FREQUENCY (In minutes)	SERVICE No. and THROUGH FARE	
SEA FRONT (Aquarium) to MOULSECOOMB	4	L	(1½d.)
SEA FRONT (Aquarium) to ELM GROVE & RACE HILL	10	E	(2d.)
SEA FRONT (Aquarium) to QUEEN'S PARK	10	Q	(2d.)
SEA FRONT (Aquarium) to DITCHLING ROAD... ...	4	*D	(2d.)
SEA FRONT (Aquarium) to BEACONSFIELD ROAD ...	4	*B	(2d.)
SEA FRONT (Aquarium) to DYKE ROAD	5	C	(2d.)
SEVEN DIALS to LOWER ROCK GARDENS and RACE HILL	5	C	(2d.)
SEA FRONT to CENTRAL STATION	5	S	(1d.)

2d. from Station to any part of tram system

NOTE: * Routes D and B comprise a circular Tour of over 4 miles, occupying 30 minutes

27. We start our tour of Brighton Corporation Tramways at the Main Line Station, known as Brighton Central in tramway days. On this summer's day, the motorman of car 2 eases his charge over the points, whilst the trolley is about to resume its trailing position on the reversing wire. Note also the Morris Commercial Davigdor Dairies van and the Tilling Regent bus on the stand outside the station. (A.J.Watkins)

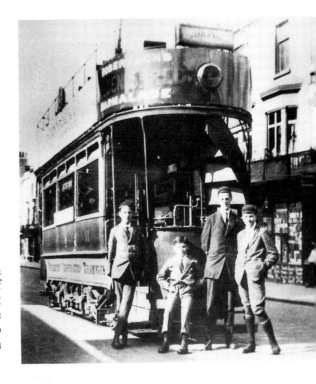

28. Looking out from the station down Queen's Road towards town, we catch sight of car 11 posed with a family group sometime just before the First World War. The four lads are smartly dressed and are, no doubt, eager to board the tram which will take them to the sea front. (R.A.Elliston Coll.)

29. An illuminated car, decorated with coloured bulbs and a crown for the King George V Jubilee in 1935, prepares to depart from the terminus. (D.W.K.Jones)

30. A crew member peers with interest at the photographer as the motorman makes final checks before leaving the single track stub terminal. (D.W.K.Jones)

31. A fine array of transport interest. Car 10 was built at the Lewes Road Depot in 1928; it is standing next to one of the distinctive Brighton taxis operated by the "Streamline Association." The vehicle itself is a Morris 14 of 1938, the same year in which the "Association" was granted sole rights by the Southern Railway for the use of the station cab rank. Finally a Brighton, Hove and District Dennis bus completes the picture. (D.W.K.Jones)

32. A final view of the station forecourt before we set off down Queen's Road towards the Aquarium terminus. In this picture the only casualty of "progress" is the tram, car 65 having met its end in 1939. At the time of writing, the Streamline Taxi firm still plies the streets and the Southern Electric trains have metamorphosed into Network SouthEast. Even OXO on the advert hoarding is still around to tempt the taste buds. (D.W.K.Jones)

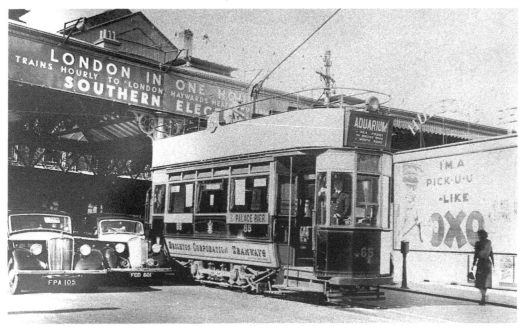

33. Decades before the entry of the UK into the European Community, Brighton was already well versed in its international role. Here we see a group of trams laid on for the "Entente Cordiale" to transport French visitors from the station. Car 18 is in its original condition with reversed stairs and mounted on a Peckham four wheel truck. Somewhat out of the ordinary, however, was the bunting and decoration with "Vive La France" picked out in red, white and blue bulbs on the upper deck decency panels. (R.J.Harley Coll.)

35. Further along Queen's Road, car 22 in original condition passes Emery's Temperance Hotel, which later became Queen's Road Hotel, its reputation matching the gradient outside... downhill all the way!...until red light status was reached. Happily for the Edwardian trippers on the top deck, this was all in the future. (R.H.Tabraham Coll.)

34. In the summer of 1938, G.E.Baddeley snapped cars 46 and 49 passing outside the Friendly Society Building seen in the previous photograph. Obviously the owners don't seem to have much luck with the tenants as the "To Be Let" board in the earlier view has now been replaced by a "For Sale" sign! (G.E.Baddeley)

36. The first central tram terminus was a loop around Victoria Gardens. Here we see cars 24 and 40 waiting for the off, whilst an Inspector checks his timetable with the motorman of car 24. (R.J.Harley Coll.)

37. A similar panorama of the terminus shows trams with black lettered indicator blinds, whilst the statue of Queen Victoria looks regally on. (R.H.Tabraham Coll.)

Corporation Tramways.   Brighton.

38. The Aquarium extension was opened in July 1904 and this postcard scene was taken shortly afterwards. As in all these early views the complete lack of competing traffic is in stark contrast to the motorised race track this area has become today. (R.J.Harley Coll.)

39. The car in the centre at the Aquarium/Old Steine still retains its Peckham truck. These were replaced from 1908 as the Manager considered they were too light to stand up to the severe work on the gradients of the town. The process took six years until the tried and tested Brill 21E carried the fleet. An ominous sign for the future is the appearance of the Milnes/Daimler bus in the right hand corner of the picture. (R.H.Tabraham Coll.)

40. Cars 31 and 44 stand with the waiting shelter behind them. Note that the trams are already liberally plastered with advertisements. This was a common practice in Great Britain, the theory being that the revenue thus obtained would pay for the annual repaint and varnish of each car. (Lens of Sutton)

41. A good view of the passenger facilities at the Old Steine. Above the shelters is emblazoned the message.... "WELCOME TO SUNNY BRIGHTON...QUEEN OF THE SOUTH." The sign would be turned on at dusk to remind visitors of the town's wholesome commitment to Sun, Sea and Sand, which were the backbone of pre-war family holidays. The actual signs were designed by students at the local Art College and there was always an argument over how much the Corporation would cough up in payment for the display! (R.A.Elliston Coll.)

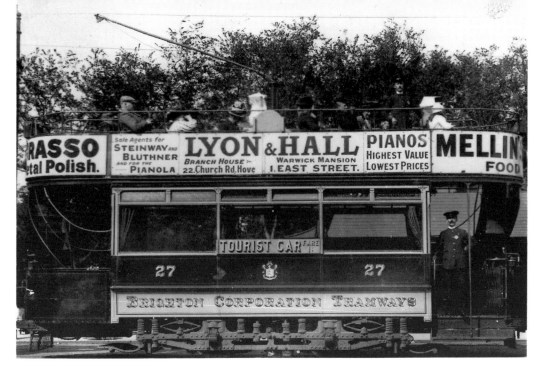

42. In 1905 Tourist Cars were introduced. The route was from the Aquarium to Dyke Road, then the car returned to Preston Circus where it reversed again to proceed round the Beaconsfield-Ditchling circular to the foot of Ditchling Road, then into Union Road across the Lewes Road tracks and up Elm Grove to the terminus at Race Hill. Here the car waited 15 minutes for the passengers, who were only allowed to ride on the top deck, to take in the extensive views of the town and the sea. A return was then made to the Aquarium; the fare for the trip was one shilling(5p.). An additional conductor was stationed on the top deck as a guide and he no doubt aided those less than fit souls who complained about having to change direction and seat three times on the journey. (R.H.Tabraham Coll.)

43. Overnight, Saturday/Sunday, 4/5th May 1929, a large number of workmen toiled in torrential rain to alter the tracks circulating the two Victoria Gardens to conform with the one way traffic scheme. The work force included men lent by the neighbouring tram systems of Southampton and Portsmouth; the whole job was completed by 9 a.m. on the Sunday morning. On the night of 30th March 1930 the tracks at the Old Steine terminus were also reversed, cars now entering from east to west, as can be seen in this 12th July 1933 view. Note the double saloon doors on car 54. In contrast, all vehicles built after 1932 had single doors to the saloon. (R.H.Tabraham Coll.)

44. Car 18 is pictured at the terminus; the date is the late thirties and the tram is still in immaculate condition. The livery of dark maroon and cream with blue shaded, gold lettering glistens in the sunshine. At night the many coloured bulbs around the top deck were illuminated. What a sad contrast with the present day when dirt and grime seem to be the fleet colours of many buses! (D.W.K.Jones)

45. Don Thompson, the well known London tramway photographer, took time off from the metropolis to visit Brighton on Sunday, 23rd October 1938. Car 40 had an unusual windscreen vestibule; the same tram was also equipped for a short time with a trolley gantry instead of the normal standard. The experiment was ended due, it was said, to complaints from top deck passengers getting spattered with grease from the contraption. No doubt, this was too much when allied to the natural dangers of receiving a direct hit from a passing seagull! (D.A.Thompson)

46. Ready to depart is car 77 on route N to Dyke Road; the route letter is displayed in the middle of the upper deck decency panel. A gentleman seems to be peering from under the centre window destination blind. Whether he was curious about the photographer or suspicious, we shall never know. At any event, on this Sunday a couple of weeks after Chamberlain's Munich agreement with Hitler, the international climate in the rest of Europe was still distinctly threatening and less than a year after this photo, anyone pointing a camera in the street would have had some explaining to do at the police station. (D.A.Thompson)

47. Rounding the corner out of the terminus, car 40 trundles away en route to Lewes Road. Notice the coloured light signals to the right of the tram, these were used to indicate the departure of different services. Previous to this a timekeeper had been employed with a very shrill whistle. (R.H.Tabraham Coll.)

48. Car 73 and trolleybus 5 line up at the Aquarium terminus shortly before the end of tramway operation. Route 26A had replaced tram route D on 1st June 1939. Car 73 which was barely nine years old , was the first tram

with roller bearings and helical gearing. All
handrails, driving controls and other parts
which on earlier cars had been polished brass,
were now chromium plated. (D.W.K.Jones)

PRESTON DROVE
26 ST. PETER'S CH
OPEN MARKET
A DITCHLING RD

5

FUF 5

49. In the last uneasy weeks of summer 1939 before the outbreak of war, the fate of the Brighton trams was fixed. Here we see a brand new A.E.C. 661T trolleybus which took over the service to Seven Dials on 17th July, replacing tram route S as far as the station. Trolleybus service 40 was very short lived, making this a rare photograph. (D.W.K.Jones)

PRESTON CIRCUS

50. The junction of Viaduct Road and Beaconsfield Road at Preston Circus under construction in 1901. Notice there is scarcely a bare head to be seen amongst the workmen. The cloth cap denotes hard physical labour with pick and shovel. (R.H.Tabraham Coll.)

51. Shortly after the opening of the system, car 11 noses gingerly across the points and out of New England Road to traverse Preston Circus. The tram will then head along London Road to the terminus at Victoria Gardens, which was shown on the indicator blind as "Pavilion." (R.H.Tabraham Coll.)

52. Looking north from Preston Circus. The centre poles in Beaconsfield Road lead the eye towards the railway viaduct where a Kemp Town train has just left London Road Station. On the nearest centre pole there is a white car stop band and on the curve from New England Road there is evidence of either a derailment or a cart with metal tyres having "used" the tramway. (R.H.Tabraham Coll.)

54. The old chemist's shop on the corner has gone, replaced in 1932 by Barclays Bank, but the semaphores with their warning bells remain. (R.H.Tabraham Coll.)

53. In the 1920 s traffic has grown considerably and movements are controlled by semaphore signals operated by a policeman in an ornamental pulpit. An illuminated tram is waiting for the right of way whilst a Tilling bus on service 5 from Patcham looks on. (R.H.Tabraham Coll.)

55. One final view of Preston Circus with, on the left, the former house of Mr.Longhurst of the Amber Pale Ale Brewery. The brewery was to the right of the picture and was demolished to ease the curve from Viaduct Road into Beaconsfield Road. A tram depot was also intended for the rest of the site, however, the underlying Wellesbourne Stream would have rendered the foundations extremely unstable. (A.J.Watkins)

BEACONSFIELD / DITCHLING ROUTES

56. A long vista of centre poles graces Beaconsfield Villas as we look down the hill towards Preston Circus. These were removed in 1923, mainly due to the number of motorists who misjudged speed and distance, and insisted on colliding with them. (R.H.Tabraham Coll.)

DITCHLING ROAD ACCIDENT

57. Another collision, this time in Ditchling Road, served to illustrate that well known law of physics the domino effect. In 1913 a steam wagon ran into one of the cast iron telephone poles and brought the whole lot down, thereby cutting the main telephone link to London. Notice that the tramway standards were made of steel, altogether sterner stuff, and had to support the telephone department's embarrassment. (R.H.Tabraham Coll.)

58. This view down Preston Drove with Preston Park in the distance, serves to illustrate some of the gradients encountered by the Brighton trams. (R.H.Tabraham Coll.)

59. A green light shows as a tram edges out over the intersection of Upper Lewes Road and Ditchling Road. At this spot on 17th September 1935, car 74 ran out of control, skidding on wet leaves blown on the track. It then struck and killed a cyclist. The unfortunate victim was a Corporation gardener and £750 was paid as compensation to his widow and family. The tram then slid further gathering speed on the gradient, and in a vain attempt to control the car, the driver reversed his controller and applied power which operated the points and diverted the car into Union Road where it overturned. (D.W.K.Jones)

DYKE ROAD ROUTE

61. The Dyke Road route was opened in its entirety on 27th July 1904 and replaced by buses on 26th April 1939. This early scene shows a tram turning from Dyke Road across Seven Dials to head down New England Road. The Goldsmit Road stub tracks and wires attest to the forlorn attempt to penetrate Hove. Alas! It was not to be and the redundant equipment had been removed by 1919. (R.H.Tabraham Coll.)

60. In the opposite direction to the previous view, car 29 has just crossed the trailing points from Viaduct Road and will shortly take the left hand facing points along Union Road. Behind the tram is the former Diocesan Teacher Training College; in front can be glimpsed one of the famous rustic tram shelters. (A.J.Watkins)

62. Another view of the corner at Seven Dials in 1938 shows car 31 about to set down passengers before the descent to Preston Circus. (G.E.Baddeley)

64. Car 56 is at the terminus and was photographed on 19th June 1935. The tram bears the route letter N and looks very smart in the maroon and primrose livery; there is time for the crew to have a chat in the lower saloon before setting off for town. (G.N.Southerden)

←――――――

63. The broad sweep of Dyke Road is typical of many British suburban streets of this era, tree-lined with middle class housing and a frequent tram service. Sometimes the lady of the house had to make sure she did not catch the same tram as the cook and the parlour maids-it was simply not good form!
(R.H.Tabraham Coll.)

65. Late autumn sunshine catches the driver of car 68 at the Dyke Road terminus. The street lighting suspended from the tramway poles would sway gently with the passing of each car; this scene captures something of the romance of the tramcar. (D.A.Thompson)

66. The return journey passes along London Road seen here shortly after the turn of the century. (R.J.Harley Coll.)

67. St.George's Place, by the Parish Church of St.Peter's was the intersection of the outbound and inbound tracks. Notice the policeman on the left keeping his eye on the tram from Lewes Road which has just pulled up at the stop in this 1906 view. (R.J.Harley Coll.)

LEWES ROAD ROUTE

68. Along the Lewes Road route, car 20 is heading for town under the impressive Kemp Town branch viaduct which was demolished in 1976. Notice the touring bike in the foreground which seems to be a fixed wheel model with only a front brake. (G.E.Baddeley)

70. Car 52 is at the same location as the previous photo. Notice the lack of windscreen and the handrails extending in front of the driver, giving him a rather caged-in look. (R.H.Tabraham Coll.)

69. The tracks in Lewes Road ended just past the depot outside Preston Barracks which were established in 1795 as Europe was on the brink of war. Route L was the first to operate in 1901 and was the only service in Brighton not bedevilled by steep gradients. Car 37 waits at the terminus whilst a crew member has a quick cigarette. (R.H.Tabraham Coll.)

LEWES ROAD DEPOT

71. Outside the depot in Lewes Road. The scene is almost the same today and the office building still retains frosted glass windows etched with the tramway undertaking's name.

Obviously the tram and the old bus have now disappeared and there is an enormous increase in modern traffic. (A.J.Watkins)

73. A closer look at the depot in the mid-thirties. The conductor is guiding the trolley pole by means of a rope attached to the trolley head. On the far left is a mirror for staff. Smartness was the order of the day; notice the two questions above the mirror. "How do I look today?...Is there room for improvement?" Woe betide any crew member who turned up to work unshaven or wearing brown shoes with navy trousers! (R.H.Tabraham Coll.)

←

72. A depot panorama taken after 1928. In the foreground is a fine selection of tramway impedimenta including stacks of rails, traction standards and ornamental bases, night watchman's huts and piles of granite setts removed during road resurfacing. On the left a three-wheel dumper truck is carrying around odds and ends. (R.A.Elliston Coll.)

74. The depot yard again, with tram scrapping in full swing. Some trolleybus overhead has been erected and car 14 stands with others forlornly off the rails like mourners at their own funeral. (D.W.K.Jones)

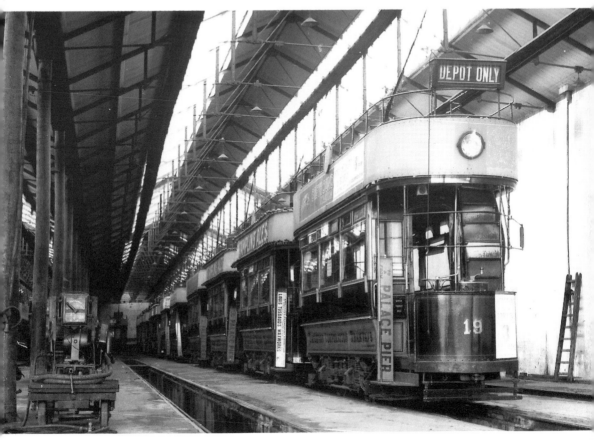

76. A line of cars with "Palace Pier" slipboards waits for service. Open maintenance pits were commonplace throughout the country. They were mostly filled in after the trams were scrapped, as hauling out a bus from a six foot pit was a major task. The leading car displays a destination which subsequently had a minor role in Graham Greene's famous novel of 1938, "Brighton Rock." (D.W.K.Jones)

75. Car 1 is seen with a prophetic notice on the dash. The fate of all trams was as part exchange for a new transport system. There were critics of the Corporation's policy who pointed to the wasted investment in plant and car rebuilding; others thought the raw materials used for the conversion could have been put to more patriotic purposes at a time of impending national emergency. (D.W.K.Jones)

77. A rare shot of Brighton works car 1. It was painted in the same colours as the passenger fleet, with the name of William Marsh, Engineer & Manager below the front platform. He managed the Brighton undertaking until retirement on 31st May 1939; he was a great believer in trams and his "evolutionary" policy of car rebuilding had kept the wheels turning. (D.W.K.Jones)

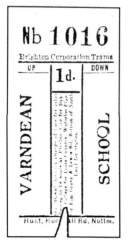

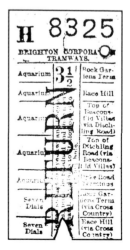

ELM GROVE ROUTE

78. The Lewes Road tracks are in the foreground as a tram descends Elm Grove past one of the remaining centre poles. On the far right of the picture are the town's only remaining almshouses, built in 1795 for six poor widows of the Church of England. (G.E.Baddeley)

79. Further up Elm Grove opposite Wellington Road a tram bound for Seven Dials on route C slows to stop. Much criticism was directed against trams because intending passengers had to step out into the road. However, there is a marked lack of other vehicles in this late twenties view. (A.J.Watkins)

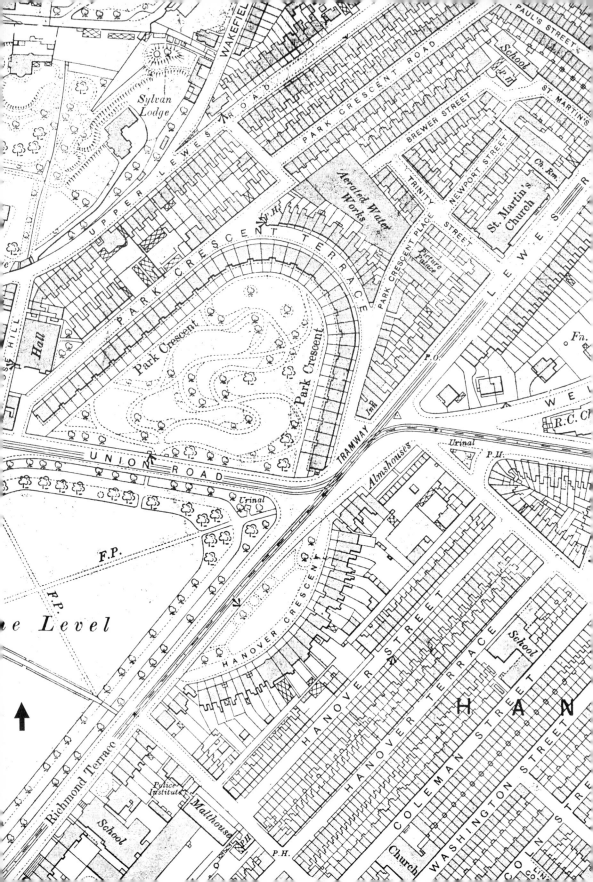

80. The camera angle on this shot of Elm Grove gives no indication of the gradient encountered by car 26 as it heads towards Queen's Park. (R.A.Elliston Coll.)

81. Car 11 has just arrived from Queen's Park Road and is reversing on Elm Grove to continue cross-country on route C. Car 2 waits to proceed down the hill on route E to the Aquarium. (R.A.Elliston Coll.)

82. On 8/9/10th August 1939, the last peacetime Brighton Races were held. Although the new overhead was up along Elm Grove, the trolleybus service was not ready and 40 extra trams had to reopen the Station route to cope with the influx of punters. Here we see some of the cars waiting to return to town; scenes such as this recall the heyday of trams in Great Britain. (C.Carter)

84. A tram with "Pavilion" on the destination blind is passed by a Jaguar SS 1.5 litre model. The Pavilion in Brighton is the well known tourist attraction and architectural flight of fancy built for the Prince Regent in 1787 and completed in 1820. (C.Carter)

83. A very rare view of a Brighton tram with a headlamp blackout mask.The appearance of this and the disturbing news of troop deployments on the Polish-German frontier must have been in the minds of many who attended the race meeting. (W.J.Haynes)

85. At Elm Grove/Race Hill terminus, car 75 waits for the return journey. Notice the short metal pillar containing a departmental telephone so that an inspector could dial up extra trams to help shift crowds. (R.H.Tabraham Coll.)

86. The trolley of the 1938 enthusiasts' special tram is reversed on Race Hill. One of the distinctive passenger shelters can be seen on the left; those people standing on the top deck had a marvellous panorama of the surrounding Downs and Channel Coast. (D.W.K.Jones)

87. Car 30 having made its way down Queen's Park Road and Egremont Place comes to rest at the terminus in Upper Rock Gardens. It will then reverse and return to the Aquarium by a very circuitous route. A glance at the map will confirm that, as the crow flies, the two termini were only a few hundred yards apart. (R.A.Elliston Coll.)

88. An earlier view of the terminus shows a very solid bracket arm traction standard in the middle of the road. Later this and the centre poles in the distance were deemed a traffic hazard; they were replaced by the normal pavement standard and span wire construction. (R.A.Elliston Coll.)

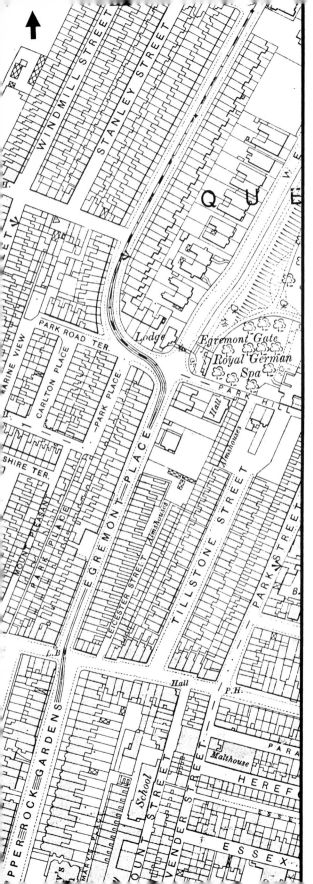

89. The route was converted to trolleybuses on 31st August 1939. Car 74 still looks in fine fettle as it lays over beneath the new trolleybus wires which curve into St.James's Street. The replacing vehicles on circular services 41/42 were thus enabled to reach the Old Steine by the shortest route. (C.Carter)

90. The Brighton trams are preserved in miniature by this fine model constructed by Ray Tabraham to a scale of 1:12. The car incorporates all the detail of the prototype pictured previously. (R.H.Tabraham)

91. The tram shelters for intending passengers were an attractive design, halfway between a country cottage and a garden shed, which an architect might refer to as "rustic tramway vernacular!" They were stained and varnished a glossy medium oak; inside on the sloping ceiling opposite the passenger bench were several posters including normally one from the Temperance Society. Most trams latterly carried advertising for Tamplins Ales; nobody, it seems, thought it a conflict of interests! The bus in the picture is a Leyland PD2/37 delivered in 1961 and seen at Dyke Road terminus on tramway replacement service 51. (R.H.Tabraham)

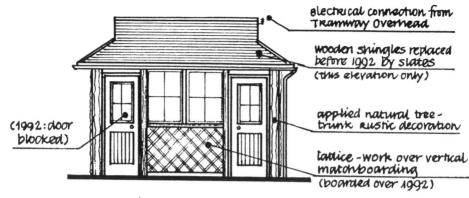

electrical connection from Tramway Overhead

wooden shingles replaced before 1992 By slates (this elevation only)

applied natural tree-trunk rustic decoration

(1992: door blocked)

lattice-work over vertical matchboarding (boarded over 1992)

Elevation to Ditchling Road

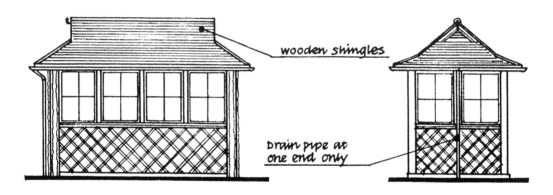

wooden shingles

Drain pipe at one end only

Elevation to Pavement

Elevation towards Brighton (south) (other elevation identical)

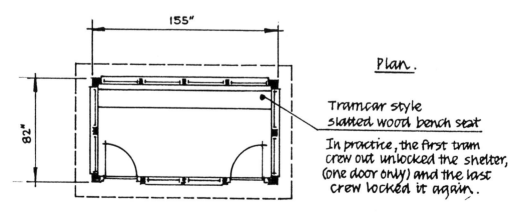

155"

82"

Plan.

Tramcar style slatted wood bench seat

In practice, the first tram crew out unlocked the shelter, (one door only) and the last crew locked it again.

Brighton Corporation Transport Tramcar Shelter, Ditchling Road. The Dyke Road Shelter is similar. Scale: 4mm = 1ft. Drawn by J.D.Bolton OSB.

The next six pictures are of representatives of each class of tram in Brighton. There were minor variations within a particular class, caused as a result of a rebuilding programme which covered the whole fleet.

92. CLASS A. Single truck, open top cars delivered 1901-1904 with reversed stairs and two 30 HP motors. Car 20 is seen here on the depot fan in Lewes Road. Notice also the lattice platform gate, the double bulkhead doors and the wire mesh lifeguard.
(R.A.Elliston Coll.)

93. CLASS B. From 1908 onwards, cars were retrucked on the Brill 21E. Later changes included direct stairs and wooden slatted lifeguards; the original reason for the reversed staircase was the safety of passengers as they ascended so that they were not suddenly thrown off the back of the car as the driver accelerated. This problem was more apparent than real; in practice, the driver's field of vision was impaired especially on the near side between the tram and the kerb. In all, 57 class B cars were built between 1914 and 1926 at the depot workshops. (D.A.Thompson)

94. CLASS C. Eight cars were built in 1926/7 and were fitted with vestibule windscreens on slightly extended platforms to accommodate the throw of the handbrake. (D.A.Thompson)

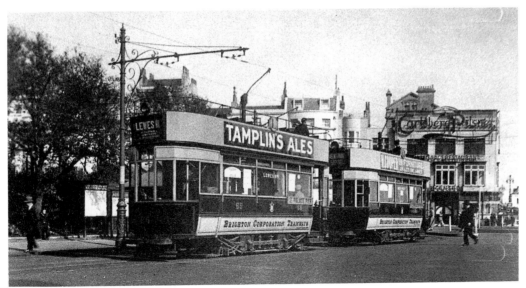

95. CLASS D. New convex side panels appeared on these trams, resulting in a wider lower deck containing upholstered seats and backs rather than the original wooden benches. Seven cars were built between 1928 and 1932 with two 40HP motors and compressed air brakes. (D.W.K.Jones)

96. CLASS E. Car 72 was one of thirteen built between 1929 and 1931; from 1933 these trams were fitted with SKF roller bearings. They had two 50HP motors and smaller 26ins/660mm. diameter wheels. As in the previous class, the indicator box was now situated just above the windscreen in the upper deck decency panel. (D.W.K.Jones)

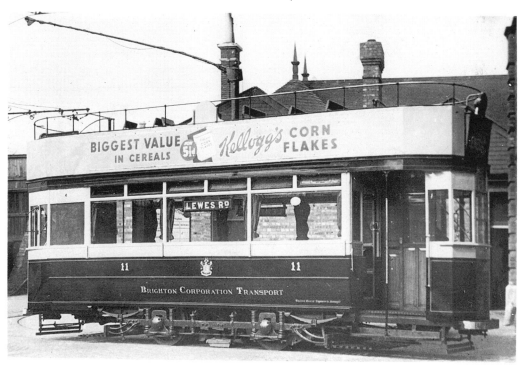

97. CLASS F. The final thirty-two cars, built between 1932 and 1937 were painted in a modified livery and from 1936 the word "Transport" replaced "Tramways" on the side panel. Stairway doors and cupboards were standard, as were deeper upper deck panels on the later cars. Chromium fittings replaced brass handles and rails; the chore of polishing brass on the older cars was too labour intensive, hence the change.
(Tramway Museum Society)

Brill 21E truck

Peckham truck

BRIGHTON CORPORATION TRAMWAYS.

REDUCTION OF FARES

ON AND AFTER

MONDAY, JAN. 4th, 1926

The following Fares will apply in either direction:

ORDINARY FARES.

Ditchling & Beaconsfield Rd. CIRCULAR ROUTES.

1d. Fares.

Aquarium to the Fountain.
Fountain to St. Saviour's Church.
Oxford Street to Rugby Road.
St. Saviour's Church to Top of Ditchling Road.
Top of Ditchling Road to Top of Beaconsfield Villas.
Top of Beaconsfield Villas to Stanford Avenue (at Florence Road).
Stanford Avenue (at Florence Road) to the Fountain.

1½d. Fares.

Aquarium to College.
College to Top of Ditchling Road.
Top of Beaconsfield Villas to Preston Circus.
Preston Circus to the Aquarium.

2d. Fares.

Aquarium to Rugby Road.
Pavilion to Top Ditchling of Road (via Ditchling Road).
College to Top of Beaconsfield Villas.
Rugby Road to Stanford Avenue (at Florence Road).
Top of Ditchling Road to Preston Circus.
Top of Beaconsfield Villas to Pavilion (via Beaconsfield Road).
Stanford Avenue (at Florence Road) to the Aquarium.

2½d. Fares.

Aquarium to Top of Ditchling Road (via Ditchling Road).
Fountain to Top of Beaconsfield Villas (via Ditchling Road).
College to Stanford Avenue (at Florence Road).
Rugby Road to Preston Circus.
Top of Ditchling Road to the Fountain (via Beaconsfield Road).
Top of Beaconsfield Villas to the Aquarium.

3d. Fares.

Aquarium to Top of Beaconsfield Villas (via Ditchling Road).
Top of Ditchling Road to Aquarium (via Beaconsfield Road).

RETURN FARES.

3d. 'Short' Return Tickets.

Aquarium to Rugby Road.
Aquarium to Stanford Avenue (at Florence Road).

4d. 'Long' Return Tickets.

Aquarium to Top of Ditchling Road (via Ditchling Road).
Aquarium to Top of Beaconsfield Villas (via Beaconsfield Road).

Lewes Road Route.

1d. Fares.

Aquarium to the Fountain.
Fountain to St. Paul's Street.
Bottom of Elm Grove to the Arches.
St. Paul's Street to Lewes Rd. Terminus

1½d. Fare.

Aquarium to Bottom of Elm Grove.

2d. Fares.

Aquarium to the Arches.
Fountain to Lewes Road Terminus.

2½d. Fare.

Aquarium to Lewes Road Terminus.

RETURN FARES.

3d. "SHORT" RETURN TICKET.

Aquarium to Lewes Road Arches.

4d. "LONG" RETURN TICKET.

Aquarium to Lewes Road Terminus.

Elm Grove & Queen's Park Rd. Routes.

1d. Fares.

Aquarium to the Fountain.
Fountain to De Montfort Road.
Bottom of Elm Grove to Queen's Park Junction.
Queen's Park Junction to Race Hill or Pepper Box.
Down Terrace to Egremont Gate.
Albion Hill to Rock Gardens.

1½d. Fares.

Aquarium to Bottom of Elm Grove.
Bottom of Elm Grove to Race Hill or Pepper Box
Down Terrace to Rock Gardens.

2d. Fares.

Aquarium to Bonchurch Road.
Fountain to Race Hill or Pepper Box.
Bottom of Elm Grove or Race Hill to Rock Gardens.

2½d. Fares.

Aquarium to Race Hill or Pepper Box
Fountain to Rock Gardens.

3d. Fare.

Aquarium to Rock Gardens.

RETURN FARES.

3d. "SHORT" RETURN TICKETS.

Aquarium to Bonchurch Road.
Rock Gardens to Bonchurch Road or Race Hill.

4d. "LONG" RETURN TICKET.

Aquarium to Race Hill or Pepper Box.

5d. RETURN TICKET.

Aquarium to Rock Gardens.

Dyke Road Route.

1d. Fares.

Aquarium to the Fountain.
Fountain to Preston Circus.
Preston Circus to Seven Dials.
Seven Dials to Port Hall Road.
Port Hall Road to The Drove.
The Drove to Dyke Road Terminus.

1½d. Fare.

Aquarium to Preston Circus.
Seven Dials to Dyke Road Drive.
Port Hall Road to Dyke Road Terminus.

2d. Fares.

Aquarium to Seven Dials.
Fountain to Port Hall Road.
Preston Circus to Dyke Road Drive.
Seven Dials to Dyke Road Terminus.

2½d. Fares.

Aquarium to Port Hall Road.
Fountain to Dyke Road Drive.
Preston Circus to Dyke Road Terminus.

3d. Fare.

Aquarium to Dyke Road Terminus.

RETURN FARES.

3d. "SHORT" RETURN TICKETS.

Aquarium to Seven Dials.
Seven Dials to Dyke Road Terminus.

4d. "LONG" RETURN TICKET.

Aquarium to Port Hall Road.

5d. RETURN TICKET.

Aquarium to Dyke Road Terminus.

Station Route.

1d. Fares.

Aquarium to Top of North Road.
Pavilion to the Station.

1½d. Fare.

Aquarium to the Station.

THROUGH FARES TO AND FROM THE STATION.

The change of Cars to be made at Bottom of North Road only.

2d. Bonchurch Rd., Lewes Rd. Arches, Rugby Rd., Stanford Av. (at Florence Rd.) and Seven Dials to Railway Station.

2½d. Race Hill, Pepper Box, Lewes Rd. Terminus, Top of Ditchling Rd. (via Ditchling Rd.), Top of Beaconsfield Villas (via Beaconsfield Rd.), and Port Hall Rd. to the Railway Station.

3d. Rock Gardens, Chester Terrace, and Dyke Road Terminus to the Railway Station.

MISCELLANEOUS FARES.

DYKE RD. AND BEACONSFIELD RD. THROUGH FARES.

Change of Cars to be made at Preston Circus only.

2d. Seven Dials to Stanford Avenue (at Florence Road).
2½d. Seven Dials to Top of Beaconsfield Villas.
3d. Seven Dials to Top of Ditchling Road.

DYKE RD., LEWES RD., ELM GROVE THROUGH FARES.

Change of Cars to be made at the Fountain only

2d. Seven Dials to Bottom of Elm Grove.
3d. Seven Dials to Race Hill or Lewes Road Terminus.

CROSS COUNTRY FARES ON THROUGH CARS ONLY.

2d. Preston Circus to Race Hill or Lewes Rd. Terminus. | **3d.** Seven Dials to Race Hill or Lewes Road Terminus.

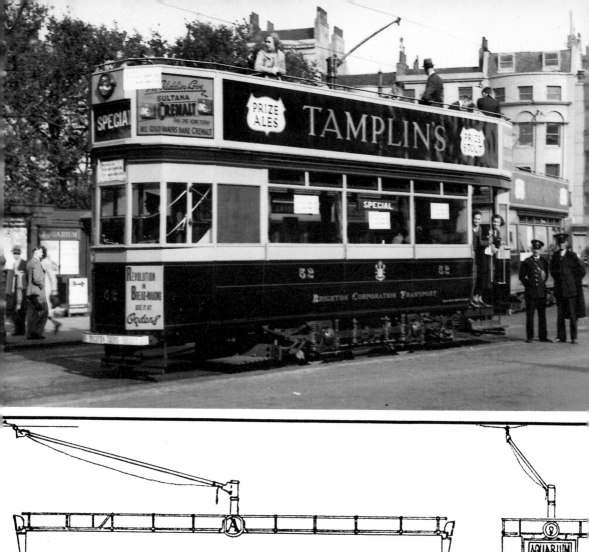

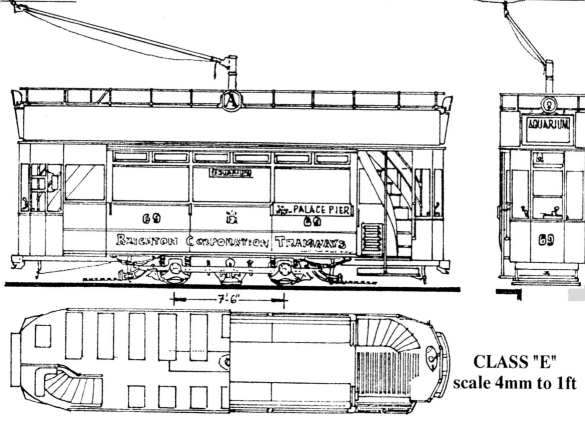

CLASS "E"
scale 4mm to 1ft

UPPER | LOWER

98. A final view of car 52 on the 1938 Tram Tour. This car was the last of a trio outshopped by the Corporation in 1937. It was the last completely new open top double decker built in this country, recent heritage replicas excepted, and it had an active life of barely two years. The official description of the livery was "Burgundy and Cream." Other observers have variously described it as "Dark Maroon and Primrose," or "Deep Chocolate Brown and Cream." (D.W.K.Jones)

99. The cosy interior of car 52. Saloon seating in earlier class F cars consisted, on each side, of three double transverse seats (rotating), a longitudinal seat for 4/5, and one single transverse (rotating). This was extremely comfortable, but was found to increase considerably the loading/unloading time at each stop. Therefore, in later years the three double transverse seats were replaced by extending the longitudinal seats, as seen in the picture. (D.W.K.Jones)

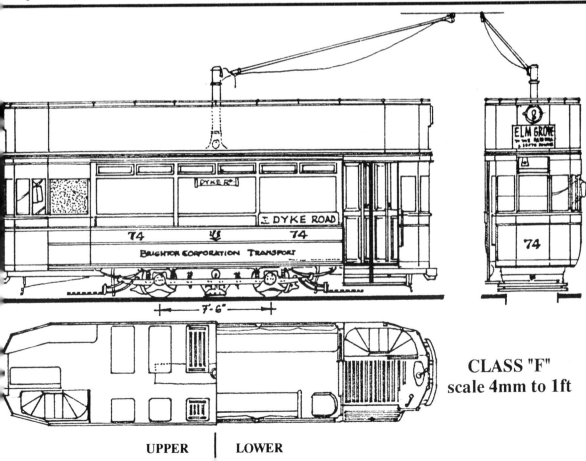

CLASS "F"
scale 4mm to 1ft

UPPER | LOWER

100. THE END. The last car draws up in front of the depot at around 2 a.m. on 1st September 1939; some of the replacing trolleybuses are parked behind this group of "last-nighters." At the same time, many miles to the East, the altogether larger nightmare of World War II was already starting.
(Brighton and Hove Gazette)

102. The line attracted the attention of contemporary artists, after all it was a British record for Brighton, the very first electric railway. This, and the following picture overleaf, depict the front and the tunnel of the extension to Paston Place under the ill fated Chain Pier which was soon destroyed in a gale. The railway's fame spread and the Dublin Express of 3rd June 1884 was suitably impressed, it wrote..."The absence of all noise, dust, smoke or effort adds, in an appreciable degree, to the sense of perfect rest; and Electric Railways will, before long, be one of the essentials of every aspiring watering place."
(J.Baker Coll.)

101. Magnus Volk stands proudly on the left hand platform of the first car of his brand new electric railway. The time is 12 noon on Saturday, 4th August 1883 and the invited guests are about to experience a totally unfamiliar sensation of being transported without any visible means of propulsion. We can only imagine the unease felt by some of these pioneer passengers. The car itself was fed with 50 volts via the two rails set at a gauge of 2ft/610mm. The railway was a great success and on the following Bank Holiday, the little 10 seat car was shuttling up and down at a maximum of 6 mph/10 kph for over 11 hours over the quarter mile track to the Chain Pier. (A.J.Watkins Coll.)

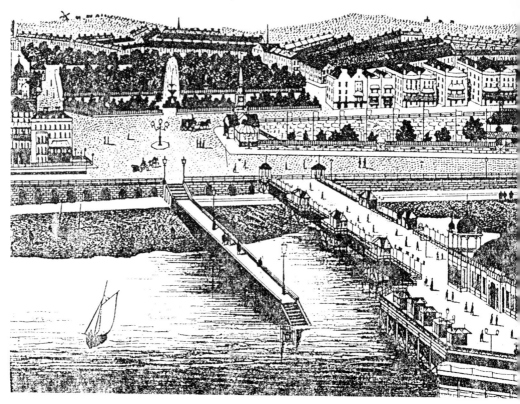

103. In 1884 the track was reconstructed to a gauge of 2ft 9ins/838mm and the line was extended by the side of Madeira Drive as depicted in this Edwardian postcard. The picture also shows the flat metal strip electric conductor which replaced the original two rail current system. One of the most famous early passengers was the 10 year old Winston Churchill who was at school in Brunswick Road in 1885. He recalls in a letter to his mother that he conversed with the driver of the Volk's car about the prospects of his father, Lord Randolph, becoming Prime Minister. (R.J.Harley Coll.)

104. Life did have its disadvantages for the infant VER; one of the most destructive was the winter gales which battered the line. After a particularly bad storm in December 1896 a complete reconstruction was necessary, as much of the right of way had vanished totally. (R.J.Harley Coll.)

105. This view shows the car sheds by Paston Place in September 1964. The third rail for the electric pick up had been installed in 1896, and before reopening in 1948 after wartime closure, all the running and current rails were renewed in a heavier section. Paston Place was the eastern terminus of the 1884 line and from 1896 passengers could change to the Seashore Tramroad to continue their journeys to Rottingdean. In 1901 a further final extension was constructed by the VER to reach Black Rock. (R.J.Harley)

106. Volk's cross bench car 9 pictured here at Paston Place in 1951 originally came from Southend-on-Sea in Essex, where it ran up and down the famous mile long pier.The car is painted in the earlier dark brown livery which was replaced in 1962 by a brighter combination of yellow and brown. (G.E.Baddeley)

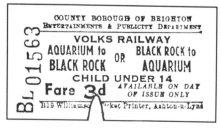

107. Eastwards from the car sheds a viaduct was constructed to enable the line to turn inland on a roadside location adjacent to Madeira Drive. Here we see a cross bench car full of 1920's holidaymakers, who from the look of them were experiencing a rather dull, chilly day in what used to be a typical British summer. (A.J.Watkins)

108. The sun is out and happy families are pottering about on the beach whilst an electric car passes above them. At this spot today the viaduct has been completely engulfed by the shingle so that the overhead railway aspect has been lost. (J.Baker Coll.)

109. Passing loops are a feature of single track operation the world over and the wait for the car coming in the opposite direction was commonplace on British tramways. The

110. Half a century has passed since the previous photograph, but the spirit of the VER lives on, only the trippers seem less formally dressed. Of interest in this 1964 view is the driver using the roof mounted controller with the large horizontal handbrake wheel in front of him. As is usual in Great Britain, all cars take the left track in the loop. (R.J.Harley)

beflagged changing vans, the horse drawn carriage and the smart attire of the visitors all add interest to this animated scene. (A.J.Watkins Coll.)

111. A view of the Aquarium terminus in its original double track state. Before the mid-sixties cars ran singly, thereby necessitating this type of terminal arrangement. In recent years two car unit operation has become standard and the second track has become disused. (G.E.Baddeley)

112. A final view of the Volk's Electric Railway at the eastern terminus of Black Rock. This picture, taken in 1951, shows a car leaving on the return journey to Central Brighton. Notice in those days a complete lack of parked cars, buses and coaches which now festoon this area in the holiday season. In 1982 the station was renamed Marina in honour of a large, unattractive, concrete complex which now dominates the shoreline hereabouts. This is one aspect of progress, I suppose, although we must be grateful that the VER, once in the vanguard of modernity, has defied the scrappers and is still going strong today. (G.E.Baddeley)

113. The Brighton and Rottingdean Seashore Electric Tramroad was unique...a world first (and last!!) for Great Britain. Here is "Pioneer" pictured in all its splendour at the Gloucester Railway Carriage & Wagon Co. works. It weighed 40 tons/ 40.6 tonnes and according to the report in "Engineering" of 4 December 1896 had the following dimensions. Length of car (bow to stern) was 45ft/13.7 metres; width (port to starboard) was 22ft/6.7 metres. On the main deck the saloon measured 25x12ft/7.6 x 3.6 metres. All this was supported on four braced steel legs, each measuring 23ft/7 metres. The bogie truck at the end of each leg contained four wheels of a uniform diameter of 33ins /838mm. The livery of the saloon was light brown and white, with the legs and bracing girders painted black.
(GRCW official photograph)

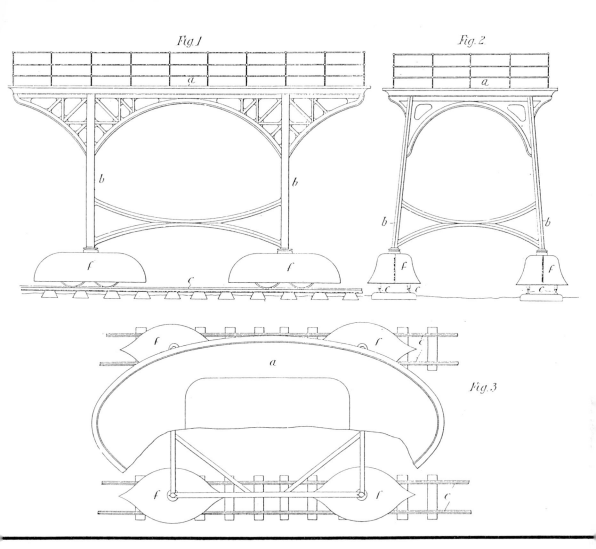

Fig.1   *Fig.2*

Fig.3

114. Not surprisingly, many views were taken on opening day; this one shows the vehicle fitted out with curtains and potted plants in the lower saloon, along which ran a plushly upholstered seat. Also notice a unique accessory to a British tramcar, the lifeboat, which thankfully was never needed...from the size of it, it would certainly have been "Women and Children Only!" (A.J.Watkins Coll.)

115. The flags are out for the first trip. This shows the pier by Banjo Groyne at the Brighton end of the enterprise. Also shown clearly is the double trolley pick up with swivel trolley heads connected to a single overhead wire at a pressure of 500 volts. (A.J.Watkins Coll.)

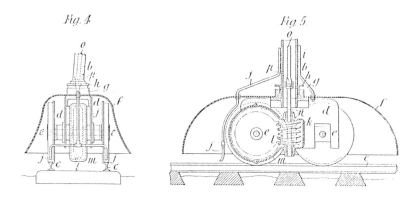

Fig. 4   Fig. 5.

Figure 1 is a side elevation of a carriage or vehicle for a sea-shore railway, constructed according to my invention.

Figure 2 is an end elevation of the same ; and,

Figure 3 is a sectional plan.

Figures 4 and 5 are transverse and longitudinal sections respectively of one of the legs of the carriage together with the travelling wheels, driving mechanism and the casing surrounding the same.

a is the deck or platform of my improved carriage which is supported upon four legs *b*, *b*, suitably braced and tied together and each preferably carried upon a four-wheel bogie, which four-wheel bogies necessitate the use of two pairs of rails *c*, *c*, namely, one pair for each side of the carriage.

d, *d* are the bogie frames, *e*, *e* are the wheel axles, and *f*, *f* are the casings or bells which surround the bogies, the said casings being hermetically fixed to the castings *g* at the upper part of the bogie frame, which castings also serve to carry the legs *b*, *b*.

In order to permit of the movements of the bogies relatively with the legs *b*, *b* and at the same time to prevent the entrance of water between the legs and the castings, a stuffing box is formed in each casting *g* and a packing gland *h* arranged in conjunction therewith (as shewn most clearly in Figures 4 and 5) the lower ends of the legs being made vertical to permit of the application of such stuffing boxes and glands.

By making the casings *f* practically air-tight as described, they act similarly to a diving bell and thus prevent the water from rising up inside the casings and carrying sand or the like into the axle bearings, and the wheels from churning up the water. To provide for any possible leakage of air from these casings I place an air pump on the carriage and adapt it to be actuated by the machinery which drives the carriage, a tube *i* being led from the pump to each casing. The said casings are brought down as closely as possible to the rails so as to act as guards and to remove obstructions from the rails and they are also preferably provided with sharp edges fore and aft so as to facilitate their free passage through the water ; the legs *b*, *b* are also advantageously similarly provided with sharp edges.

In cases where a sandy or muddy deposit covers the rails, I provide a pump for forcing streams of water through pipes *j* on to the tops of the rails, such streams of water washing off any deposit and thus leaving clean surfaces for the wheels to travel upon.

k is the worm and *l* the worm wheel through which motion is communicated to one of the bogie axles, and *m* is the casing which affords bearings for the shaft *n* of the worm and which contains oil for effecting the proper lubrication of the parts. *o* is the shaft which connects the motor upon the deck of the carriage to the worm shaft *n* ; the connection between the shafts *o* and *n*, as shewn, being effected by means of a universal joint *p* in order to allow of the inclination of the legs.

116. A few days after opening, the car and the track were wrecked in a storm. The rebuilt car had its legs extended by some 2ft/610mm and was equipped with awnings for protection of the outside passengers. The tide has risen in this picture and "Pioneer" sets off at a stately rate on the three mile voyage to Rottingdean Pier. (A.J.Watkins Coll.)

117. Construction of the tramroad started in 1894 and one wonders whether H.G.Wells, who was a frequent visitor to Sussex and the South Coast in this period, derived some of his inspiration for the malevolent Martian machines bestriding the ocean in "War of the Worlds" from the sea- going tramcar. Anyway, the two little girls in this picture seem suitably awestruck as "Pioneer" with its cargo of gentry sails past. (R.J.Harley Coll.)

118. One of the traction standards supporting the overhead can be seen to the left of the car. "Engineering" states that the support poles were either of wood or steel. The 500 volt current was returned by the four running rails and of course the sea! Certain local doctors were said to recommend swimming near the car for its "stimulating and curative properties". Notice the motorman at the "helm" of the car, standing under the lifeboat; although a ship's bell was carried, copies of the Captain's log have yet to surface! (R.J.Harley Coll.)

119. An intermediate landing stage was constructed at Ovingdean Gap; after closure, "Pioneer" was roped to the pier and this picture shows it being dismantled about 1909. The sailing barge is probably taking away the scrap materials. Only a few years earlier, the "Daddy-Long-Legs" must have been a splendid sight as it progressed past this chalk cliff landscape. (R.J.Harley Coll.)

Pier & Beach, Rottingdean.   W 4221.

120. The end of the line with an impressive triangular buffer stop to prevent "Pioneer" from making an escape towards France. The Power House underneath the pier deck can clearly be seen, it consisted of a GEC 60 kilowatt generator powered by a steam engine which developed 110 brake horsepower. (J.Baker Coll.)

121. The pier at Rottingdean some years after the service had ceased. The generating equipment has been removed and the pier and rails will shortly follow, sold to a German scrap firm. One wonders whether the two children investigating the landward track were ever able to see "Pioneer"...the unlikely vehicle "half tramcar, half penny steam boat" which had briefly graced the South Coast. (R.J.Harley Coll.)

Other Middleton Press books featuring aspects of Brighton's history -

BRIGHTON TO EASTBOURNE

BRIGHTON TO WORTHING

THREE BRIDGES TO BRIGHTON

STEAMING THROUGH WEST SUSSEX

WEST SUSSEX RAILWAYS IN THE 1980s

BATTLE OVER SUSSEX 1940

MILITARY DEFENCE OF WEST SUSSEX

Write or telephone for our latest list of local history and transport books

Easebourne Lane, Midhurst, West Sussex, GU29 9AZ
Tel: (0730) 813169   Fax: (0730) 812601